Published by Creative Education
123 South Broad Street, Mankato, Minnesota 56001
Creative Education is an imprint of The Creative Company

Art direction by Rita Marshall
Production design by The Design Lab

Photographs by China Span (Keren Su), John Giustina, Tyrrell Mendis

**Library of Congress Cataloging-in-Publication Data**

Franzen, Lenore.
Giant pandas / by Lenore Franzen.
p. cm. — (Let's investigate)
Summary: Describes the physical characteristics, behavior, habitat,
and life cycle of the giant panda, an endangered animal that now lives
in only six isolated mountain ranges in western China.
ISBN 1-58341-233-6
1. Giant panda—Juvenile literature. [1. Giant panda. 2. Pandas.
3. Endangered species.] I. Title. II. Series.
QL737.C214 F725        2002
599.789—dc21        2001047895

First edition

2  4  6  8  9  7  5  3  1

# GIANT PANDAS

## LENORE FRANZEN

Creative ● Education

# PANDA
## NUMBERS

*Scientists don't know how many giant pandas once lived. Even in ancient China, these animals were considered rare.*

*Above, a panda forest in western China Right, a young panda exploring a peach tree*

The giant panda is one of the most recogniz-able animals in the world—and one of the most endangered. Native only to China, about 1,000 pandas remain in the wild. Scientists consider giant pandas a type of bear. But pandas are unusual in so many ways that they belong to a separate species, or group, of mammals called *Ailuriopoda melanoleuca,* which means "black-and-white cat-foot."

# PANDA
## SKULL

*Even though the giant panda is considered a bear, its skull is different from that of a bear. The panda's skull has a shorter muzzle and is heavier and more solid.*

# PANDA
## DISGUISE

*Pandas' black ears look almost like another set of eyes. When pandas threaten another animal, they lower their head so two pairs of eyes seem to be staring at their enemy.*

**Pandas are covered with distinctive black and white patches**

## PHYSICAL FEATURES

Giant pandas are best known for their coloring. White covers their face, neck, rump, and tail. Their ears, shoulders, and legs are black, as is the area around their eyes. The Chinese call them *bei-shung*, or "white bear." Pandas' bold color pattern helps them spot one another at a distance and avoid unwanted encounters. During the short breeding season, their coloring may also help them find a mate quickly.

*Giant pandas are pigeon-toed and waddle when they walk. But they are good swimmers and climb trees easily.*

**Even young pandas can climb quite high**

An adult panda is as big as a black bear. It weighs 165 to 300 pounds (74–135 kg) and stands five to six feet (1.5–1.8 m) tall. Males are usually larger than females.

# PANDA

## TRACTION

*Pandas don't slip and slide on the snow and ice because thick hair covering their paws provides good traction.*

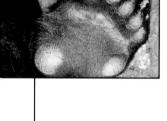

*Above, the bottom of a panda paw Right, the panda's "false thumb"*

O f French origin, the word *panda* means "bamboo-eater." Bamboo is a kind of grass with a woody, hollow stalk. In many ways, a panda's body is well designed for such a diet. Pandas' front paws have a sixth "digit" that allows them to grasp the bamboo. This "false thumb" is actually part of the wrist bone. It measures about one and a half inches (3.8 cm) in length and is covered with tough flesh. Monkeys and apes are the only other animals that can grasp things this way.

## PANDA TEETH

*Pandas have 42 large teeth that are ideally suited for grinding tough, woody bamboo stalks.*

## PANDA GROOMING

*To clean themselves, pandas comb dirt out of their fur with their claws, lick their fur, and scratch themselves. They also roll on the ground and rub soil on their bellies to absorb body oils.*

Pandas also have powerful jaws and large, ridged teeth for crunching through hard, woody bamboo stalks. Their esophagus, the tube leading to the stomach, has a thick lining to protect it from splinters. Even a panda's stomach wall is tough and muscular.

*Tough bamboo stalks snap easily between a panda's teeth*

# PANDA

## JOURNEY

*When bamboo is available, pandas don't have to travel far to get a meal. Many days they may walk only 600 feet (183 m), the length of two football fields.*

One organ in a panda's body, however, makes bamboo difficult to digest. The intestine, which helps break food down, is short in pandas. Plants such as bamboo need time to be processed by the body. Bamboo passes through a panda's short intestine so quickly that the food isn't completely digested, and the **nourishment** is lost. Pandas spend 12 hours or more per day eating bamboo, but their bodies don't benefit from most of what they consume.

*Pandas love bamboo and spend the bulk of their days feeding on bamboo stalks*

# PANDA
## EYES

*A panda's eyes are sensitive to light and have vertical pupils. which help the animal see at night when it is feeding.*

# PANDA
## SENSES

*Pandas have poor eyesight. They rely on their keen sense of smell and hearing to warn them of danger.*

# PANDA
## KILLERS

*In China, a person convicted of killing a giant panda is sentenced to life in prison.*

# PANDA
## HOME

*When a panda isn't eating or looking for food, it sleeps wherever it is. Pandas don't have a specific den or cave they consider home.*

*The mountainous terrain and dense forests of Sichuan, China*

## WHERE PANDAS LIVE

Giant pandas once ranged over much of China, neighboring Tibet, and western Burma. As the climate became drier and people cleared more land for farming and towns, pandas moved into higher elevations, where bamboo was plentiful. Today, pandas live in six isolated mountain ranges in western China's Gansu, Shaanxi, and Sichuan Provinces.

These remote, forested areas are 8,500 to 11,500 feet (2,591–3,505 m) above sea level, where the air is very thin. Panda blood is specially adapted to carry extra oxygen so the animal can survive at these high **altitudes**. Temperatures rarely rise above 68 °F (20 °C) and may drop to 19 °F (–7 °C) in winter. Snow covers the ground from fall to early spring, and the short summers are rainy and wet.

# PANDA
## PELTS

*Before pandas were an endangered species, Chinese farmers hunted and killed them so they could use the pelts to pay their taxes.*

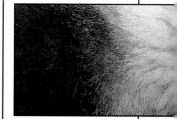

*Above, a close-up view of panda fur*
*Left, China's snow-covered mountains*

# PANDA

## ACROBATICS

*While most bears mark trees with their scent in an upright posture, pandas handstand against trees so they can leave their scent higher up the trunk.*

**A**t these higher altitudes, tall **conifers** grow among scattered clumps of short, slender bamboo. At lower levels, dense stands of bamboo reach 10 feet (3 m) tall among a mix of conifers and **deciduous** trees. Unlike other bears, the giant panda does not **hibernate**. Instead, it moves to lower elevations in the winter.

*A panda leaves scent upside-down against the trunk of a tree*

15

xcept when breeding, adult pandas live alone. They are shy and rarely seen. Each has a home range, where it feeds, of two to three square miles (5.2–7.8 sq km). A male's home range may overlap with those of several females. Within this range, a much smaller core area makes up the panda's actual home, usually less than a square mile (2.6 sq km). Pandas mark the boundaries of their home range by rubbing their scent glands, located under their tail, on trees and rocks. They also scratch tree bark to indicate where they live.

*Spotting a panda in the wild takes a keen eye*

# PANDA

*Like people, pandas sleep in different positions—on their backs, their fronts, their sides, and even sitting down.*

Because their habitat is so dense and remote, pandas rely on a wide range of sounds to communicate. Scientists have identified 11 distinct calls. For example, pandas moan when they want to warn others to stay away and chirp when they are excited, especially during mating. Barking serves several purposes, depending on the situation. Pandas may bark when they are alarmed or excited, but they also use this sound to tell other pandas where they are.

*Dense vegetation makes visual communication difficult, so pandas make sounds*

## FAVORITE FOODS

**G**iant pandas prefer bamboo to any other food, and it makes up 99 percent of their diet. They consume as much as 85 pounds (38 kg) of bamboo per day, about 40 percent of their average body weight! They feed mainly on the ground, at dusk and at night.

## PANDA THIRST

*Pandas get most of their water from juicy bamboo shoots. They may also lick snow. Sometimes, they dig a hole by a stream and wait for it to fill with water.*

*Above, a panda taking a drink*
*Left, baby pandas sharing bamboo*

# PANDA

## FOOD

*Only a few other animals depend on a bamboo diet for survival, including the red panda, bamboo lemurs, and bamboo rats.*

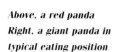

*Above, a red panda*
*Right, a giant panda in typical eating position*

When they eat, pandas usually sit down, stretching their hind legs out in front of them. They grasp a stalk, pull it down, and snap it off with their strong teeth. Holding the stalk in their front paws, they again use their teeth to strip off the tough outer part. Then, they start at one end and crunch on the bamboo, much the same way a human might eat a stalk of celery.

Pandas rely on 20 to 30 types of bamboo for their food. The most common types are arrow and umbrella. Unlike other grasses, bamboo blooms at very long intervals. Arrow bamboo, for example, flowers every 40 to 50 years. Umbrella bamboo flowers every 100 years. After it blooms, every plant of that species dies. When a **bamboo die-off** occurs, pandas must find another food source. Until new shoots appear, pandas eat flower bulbs, roots, insects, birds, rodents, and reptiles.

## PANDA
### MEDICINE

*The Chinese use different parts of the bamboo plant to treat kidney problems, reduce fevers, and cure asthma.*

## PANDA
### FAVORITE

*After a bamboo die-off, it can take a year for seeds to sprout and up to 20 years before a new crop can support a panda population.*

*Top, a developing bamboo shoot
Bottom, full-grown bamboo leaves*

# PANDA
## MATING

*When male pandas are ready to mate, they become restless. Some even bite down small trees.*

*A four-month-old giant panda cub*

## SLOW TO BREED

Female pandas breed every two to three years in the spring. They first breed when they are four or five years old. Males are usually a year or two older. Females attract males two ways. They produce deep roars, barks, and moans that can be heard far away. They also mark trees with their scent and urine. When they are ready to mate, females bleat like a goat.

About five months after mating, the female finds a den or hollow fir tree in which she gives birth to one or two cubs. A newborn cub weighs only about four to five ounces (113–142 g), about the size of an apple. That's roughly 800 times smaller than its mother—an astonishing difference.

# PANDA
## NEWBORN

*When a mother panda needs to move or get food, she uses her mouth to pick up her newborn gently by the nape and take the cub along.*

*Above, a mother panda cleaning her cub*

# PANDA
## BIRTH

**N**ewborns are pink, blind, and helpless. Their high-pitched call sounds like the cry of a human baby. They drink their mother's milk almost constantly. Because cubs need so much help at first, mothers can take care of only one at a time. Often, the second cub dies.

**A cub carried in its mother's mouth**

In the wild, about 4 out of 10 panda cubs die. The death rate for cubs in captivity is even higher.

23

I n a week, black fur begins to grow on a cub's ears, shoulders, and around the eyes. A cub opens its eyes after six or eight weeks. At three months, it weighs about 12 pounds (5.4 kg) and begins to crawl. By four months, it can walk. Gradually, the mother **weans** her cub, and by six months, it starts to eat bamboo. A cub stays with its mother until it is about 18 months old. During this time, it follows her through the forest, learning where to find the best food at different times of the year. In the wild, a panda lives about 20 years.

*At three months, cubs look like tiny versions of their parents*

# PANDA

## ENEMY

*Humans may be an adult panda's worst enemy. Some hunters risk stiff penalties in order to kill a panda and sell its fur.*

*A young panda trudging through the snow*

Even though pandas move slowly, their size and sharp claws help them defend against **predators**. But panda cubs, especially newborns, are **defenseless**. Their worst natural enemies are leopards, golden cats, and dholes, wild dogs that roam the forest in packs. Smaller predators include the weasel-like marten and the ermine.

Until the 1800s, scientists outside of China thought the red panda was the only panda in the world. Named for its fiery color, the red panda is the size of a large house cat. It resembles a raccoon, with stripes under its eyes and a bushy, ringed tail. Like the giant panda, the red panda lives alone in the same habitat, eats bamboo, and has a special wrist bone for grasping food. Some scientists group red pandas and giant pandas in their own family. Other experts place red pandas in the raccoon family.

## PANDA PATHS

*Pandas do not waste energy struggling up and down steep slopes or through the dense forest. Instead, they walk on well-worn paths made by other animals.*

25

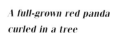

**A full-grown red panda curled in a tree**

# PANDA
## DIET

*Giant pandas in captivity are fed a varied diet of apples, carrots, rice, sweet potatoes, meat, and rye grass.*

# PANDA
## TREATS

*Giant pandas have a sweet tooth! Some have wandered down mountains and taken honey from farmers' beehives.*

*Most people have seen live pandas only in zoos*

After French missionary Père Armand David spotted a giant panda in 1869, people everywhere wanted to know more about this unusual bear. The first person to take a live panda out of China was an American named Ruth Harkness. Her husband had originally set out to capture one but died during his trip. Ruth fulfilled his dream in 1936, returning to the United States with a cub that she named Su-lin, which means "a little bit of something cute." Su-lin lived at the Brookfield Zoo near Chicago for 14 months. In 1963, the first panda was born **in captivity**, at the Beijing Zoo in China.

*The Chinese govern-
ment doesn't allow
pandas to be taken
out of the country.
But it has given pairs
of pandas to other
countries, including
Great Britain and the
United States, as
gifts of friendship.*

27

Today, about 110 giant pandas live in zoos around the world. Pandas in captivity give scientists a chance to observe their behavior and encourage breeding so the species will survive.

*A giant panda lounging
in a zoo*

# PANDA
## FOSSILS

*Fossil remains indicate that pandas have walked the earth for at least one million years.*

# PANDA
## HUNTERS

*In 1928, two sons of former U.S. president Theodore Roosevelt were the first Western hunters to shoot a giant panda. The panda was preserved and exhibited in Chicago.*

**The protected lands of Wolong Reserve in western China**

## AN UNCERTAIN FUTURE

Since 1994, the giant panda has been considered an endangered species. Loss of habitat, **poaching**, and a low **birthrate** all threaten the panda's survival. The area pandas occupy has shrunk from about 11,400 square miles (29,640 sq km) to about 5,400 square miles (14,040 sq km). A ban on commercial logging in 1998 has helped slow this loss. Pandas are also protected by law, but poaching continues.

Fortunately, in the regions where giant pandas live, China has established 33 nature **reserves**. Here pandas are safe and have plenty of bamboo. These reserves protect about 60 percent of the giant panda populations. Wolong Nature Reserve, the largest area set aside for pandas, covers about 800 square miles (2,080 sq km) in Sichuan Province. At the reserve, scientists set up a breeding station, where they hope pandas will mate.

## PANDA DEATH

*In the winter of 1975–76, more than 138 pandas died because of an umbrella bamboo die-off.*

# P A N D A
## MESSAGES

*Pandas keep in touch mainly by marking trees with their scent. These trees serve as "bulletin boards," where pandas read messages left by other pandas and then leave their own.*

**Pandas live best in their natural habitats**

The Chinese government is also planning to construct safe "corridors," or passageways, to connect the different protected areas. Using these corridors, pandas will be able to reach new feeding grounds when the bamboo in their home range dies off. They will also have access to a greater selection of potential breeding partners.

Nearly everyone recognizes giant pandas, and some people have been lucky enough to observe them in zoos. But we still have a lot to learn about this rare and endangered animal. The more we know about the giant panda, the better able we will be to ensure its survival for future generations.

*The future of the giant panda is uncertain*

# Glossary

**Altitudes** are heights or distances, usually measured in feet or meters, above sea level.

After bamboo blooms, the entire species dies. This event is called **bamboo die-off**.

A species' **birthrate** is the number of births compared to the total population over a certain period of time.

**Conifers** are trees such as pines, spruce, and firs that produce cones.

**Deciduous** trees lose their leaves at the end of the growing season. Examples include maples, oaks, and birch.

**Defenseless** animals are unable to protect themselves against predators or other threats.

To **hibernate** is to sleep or become inactive through the winter.

**In captivity** refers to animals that do not live in their natural habitat.

The energy a body gets from food is called **nourishment**.

**Poaching** is illegal hunting.

**Predators** are animals that hunt and kill other animals.

**Reserves** are protected lands on which animals can live safely.

When a mother **weans** her cub, she stops nursing it and encourages it to eat solid food.

# Index